CLOISTER

BOOKS

Cloister Books are inspired by the monastic custom of walking slowly and reading or meditating in the monastery cloister, a place of silence, centering, and calm. Within these pages you will find a similar space in which to pray and reflect on the presence of God.

This is a grace-filled book for those who are learning to swim in the deep waters of God's mercy and love—waters in which we already swim but hardly know it. Cynthia Bourgeault shows us the road to a deep and lasting hope.
—*Alan Jones*

It is unusual to encounter a book that brings together to this degree metaphysical depth, practical spirituality, and sparkling writing. True to the dynamic of the spiritual life, Cynthia Bourgeault follows the path of hope inward to the center and then back outward to the world.
—*Bruno Barnhart, OSB Cam.*

Dr. Bourgeault, an experienced guide to centering prayer, offers some profound and amazing insights into an inner joy that can be found in the midst of personal disappointment. She reveals friendship as living together in hope, which she experiences as God's "warm-heartedness."
—*Beatrice Bruteau*

Mystical Hope

MYSTICAL HOPE

Trusting in the Mercy of God

Cynthia Bourgeault

A COWLEY PUBLICATIONS BOOK

Lanham, Chicago, New York, Toronto, and Plymouth, UK

Published in the United States of America by Cowley Publications, a division of the Society of St. John the Evangelist. No portion of this book may be reproduced, stored in or introduced into a retrieval system, or transmitted, in any form or by any means—including photocopying—without the prior written permission of Cowley Publications, except in the case of brief quotations embedded in critical articles and reviews.

Library of Congress Cataloging-in-Publication Data:
Bourgeault, Cynthia.
Mystical Hope / Cynthia Bourgeault.
        p.   cm.
ISBN13: 978-1-56101-193-3
ISBN: 1-56101-193-2 (alk. paper)
1. Hope—Religious aspects—Christianity. 2. Mysticism. I. Title.
BV4638 B62 2001
248.2'2—dc 21   2001028443

Scripture quotations are from the *New International Version of the Bible.* Psalm quotations are from the Psalter in *The Book of Common Prayer (1979).*

Cover design: Vicki Black; photograph: © 2001 William Neill / www.WilliamNeill.com, *Half Dome and pine in clouds, Washburn Point, Yosemite National Park, California*

A COWLEY PUBLICATIONS BOOK

ROWMAN & LITTLEFIELD PUBLISHERS, INC.

Published in the United States of America
by Rowman & Littlefield Publishers, Inc.
A wholly owned subsidiary of The Rowman & Littlefield Publishing Group, Inc.
4501 Forbes Boulevard, Suite 200, Lanham, Maryland 20706
www.rowmanlittlefield.com

Estover Road
Plymouth PL6 7PY
United Kingdom

To Lynn Bauman
without whose encouragement and support
this book would not have been written

Contents

We awaken in Christ's body
as Christ awakens our bodies,
and my poor hand is Christ. He enters
my foot, and is infinitely me.

I move my hand, and wonderfully
my hand becomes Christ, becomes all of Him
(for God is indivisibly
whole, seamless in His Godhood).

I move my foot, and at once
he appears in a flash of lightning.
Do my words seem blasphemous?—Then
open your heart to Him

And let yourself receive the one
who is opening to you so deeply.
For if we genuinely love him,
we wake up inside Christ's body

where all our body, all over,
every most hidden part of it,

is realized in joy as Him,
and He makes us utterly real,

and everything that is hurt, everything
that seemed to us dark, harsh, shameful,
maimed, ugly, irreparably
damaged, is in Him transformed

and recognized as whole, as lovely,
and radiant in His light.
We awaken as the Beloved
in every last part of our body.

ST. SYMEON THE NEW THEOLOGIAN (949-1022)

one

Journey to the Wellsprings

What you dare not hope for—that is what He gives you.

Frère Roger, Taizé Commuity

In this short book I would like to invite you on a journey. It is a journey that may begin in despair, in hopelessness. Perhaps someone precious to you has died. You may have lost a job, a family, a lover. Perhaps you were unfairly passed over, slighted—even betrayed. You may be living under the heavy cloud of a depression that will not lift or an addiction that will not release its grip. Your life seems to be swirling downward; you do not see how to reverse the trend. There is no hope.

Hope, you feel, could help you live. It would provide a new surge of energy that would make life feel possible again. Perhaps all you need is some reassurance that the situation will change; things will get better. Perhaps it is even simpler than that: just an attitude shift, a new way of looking at things. But whatever it is, you know hope is the missing ingredient. And you want to find it.

Even if your situation is not so desperate, if the ups and downs of your life are merely the rough-and-tumble of daily living, you wonder sometimes if the roller coaster ride is really necessary. Must we be whiplashed incessantly between joy

2

and sorrow, expectation and disappointment? Is it not possible to live from a place of greater equilibrium, to find a deeper and steadier current?

The good news is that this deeper current does exist and you actually *can* find it. I hope in this book to show you how. But I should warn you from the outset that we are not going to go by the easiest route. There are plenty of books out there that can give you gimmicks, psychological techniques, comforting platitudes, and timely advice. But for me the journey to the source of hope is ultimately a *theological* journey: up and over the mountain to the sources of hope in the headwaters of the Christian Mystery. This journey to the wellsprings of hope is not something that will change your life in the short range, in the externals. Rather, it is something that will change your innermost way of seeing. From there, inevitably, the externals will rearrange.

In our usual way of looking at things, hope is tied to outcome. We would normally think of it as an optimistic feeling—or at least a willingness to go on—because we sense that things will get better in the future.

"I hope I get the job." "I hope the book contract comes through," I say to myself, idling my mind ahead to the pleasant chain of events that will be set in motion by this outcome. Or, on a darker note, "Oh, I hope it's not cancer," as I await the results of the biopsy. Suddenly the whole tapestry of joy and sadness hangs in the balance of events beyond my control, and I await the verdict with heart in mouth.

And if it should be, God forbid, that there is no cure, no way out but death or destruction, we speak of the situation as "hopeless."

The Bible knows plenty about this usual kind of hope, of course. In fact, you could almost say that the Bible is the history of one miraculous intervention of God after another to change the outcome, to create hope when things looked completely hopeless. This kind of hope is there with the Israelites at the Red Sea, seemingly between a rock and a hard place until the sea parts and the way miraculously opens. It is all over the psalms—"I love the LORD, because he has heard the voice of my supplication....I was brought very low, and he helped me" (Psalm 116:1, 5), to cite just one of about a hundred examples. It follows Jesus like a great sternwake as people flock to him for healing and new beginning. And so central is this hope to Paul's understanding of the good news in Christ that he ranks it, along with faith and love, as one of the three great theological virtues.

But where does that leave us in our own lives when the biopsy comes back malignant, when despite our fervent prayers healing does not occur, when there is no miraculous intervention? Not only is the situation still completely hopeless; even worse (if that's possible), it now seems that God has abandoned us—our religion has let us down.

Without diving yet into the middle of this anguishing conundrum, I simply want to observe that there is another kind of hope also represented in the Bible that is a complete reversal of our usual way of looking at things. Beneath the "upbeat" kind of hope that parts the sea and pulls rabbits out of hats, this other hope weaves its way as a quiet, even ironic counterpoint.

We see, it, for example, toward the end of the book of Habakkuk when, at the conclusion of a long litany of doom, the prophet suddenly exclaims—out of nowhere, it seems:

Though the fig tree does not bud
    and there are no grapes on the vines,
though the olive crop fails
    and the fields produce no food,
though there are no sheep in the pen
    and no cattle in the stalls,
yet I will rejoice in the LORD,
    I will be joyful in God my Savior.
The Sovereign LORD is my strength;
he makes my feet like the feet of a deer,
he enables me to go on the heights.
                    (Habakkuk 3:17-19)

Now here is quite a reversal! The outcome sounds about as bad as it can get: no crops, no flocks, no food—a likely sentence of starvation in this desert land. And yet Habakkuk's response is joy and strength. Not only does he vow to keep going, his survival does not even sound like a dreary, stoic sort of endurance. Instead, the prophet speaks from a lightness that seems to come flooding in upon him despite all the hopelessness of his situation. There is a spring to his step—"like the feet of a deer"—and his path leads upward, toward the heights. In the words of that lovely book title by Milan Kundera, he seems to be speaking from an "incredible lightness of being."

Jesus, too, hints at this other kind of hope in his powerful dialogue with the Samaritan woman at the well in the fourth chapter of John's gospel. The day is hot, and Jesus pauses by a well to ask a woman for a drink of water. As the two of them fall into an increasingly intense and subtle conversation, he suddenly announces, "Everyone who drinks this water will be thirsty again, but whoever drinks the water I will give him will never thirst. Indeed, the water I give him will become in him a spring of water welling up to eternal life" (John 4:13-14). What kind of water might be the continuous source of its own replenishment?

By far the most stringent "total immersion course" in this other school of hope, however, is to be found in the book of Job, which beneath its folktale framework is perhaps the most relentless pilgrimage to the wellsprings of hope in all of western literature. Under the terms of a mythical cosmic wager between God and Satan, Job's fortunes are suddenly and devastatingly upset. Wives, children, goods, even his health are all taken away. And as if this were not enough, his friends who arrive to "comfort" him set out systematically to destroy what little is left to him— his trust in a coherent universe and in his own innocence.

Yet curiously, as the story unfolds, Job's faith and hope seem to grow stronger and stronger. Far from being crushed, they take on a life of their own. As the agony of his ordeal settles into simply the way things are, and even the need to apportion blame and find coherence subsides, what seems to take wing in him is a singlehearted yearning to see God face to face, and a lyrical certainty that his redeemer lives. In one of the most extraordinary passages ever written, Job sits destitute amid the wreckage of what was once his life, and sings:

> I know that my Redeemer lives,
> and that in the end he will stand upon
> the earth.
> And after my skin has been destroyed,
> yet in my flesh I will see God.
>
> (Job 19:25-26)

Nowhere in all of literature is there such a triumphant statement of mystical hope. Certainly Job's hope is not pinned to outcome, when his whole life has collapsed and even God seems to stand against him. And yet louder and louder it sings in his soul, as if the singing itself were the hope; as if the song had been there from before the foundations of the earth.

9

The Characteristics of Mystical Hope

If we look closely at these three biblical vignettes, we might make the following observations about this other kind of hope, which we will call *mystical hope*. In contrast to our usual notions of hope:

> 1. *Mystical hope is not tied to a good outcome, to the future. It lives a life of its own, seemingly without reference to external circumstances and conditions.*

> 2. *It has something to do with* presence— *not a future good outcome, but the immediate experience of being met, held in communion, by something intimately at hand.*

3. It bears fruit within us at the psychological level in the sensations of strength, joy, and satisfaction: an "unbearable lightness of being." But mysteriously, rather than deriving these gifts from outward expectations being met, it seems to produce them from within.

10

Experiences such as this are not the exclusive provenance of the biblical world or of special people we call "saints." They belong to modern men and women as well, and occur right in the midst of daily life—far more commonly than is usually acknowledged. C. S. Lewis described these moments as being "surprised by joy." In much the same way, a friend of mine, Rosalind, describes just such a moment on a busy street in Victoria, British Columbia, a few winters ago:

It was a typical January day, dreary and cold. I was driving down Blanshard Street, half listening to the radio psychologist, half mulling over a problem in my head. A decision had been arrived at, yet part of me still wanted to hang on to doubts and self-enquiry. After being the peacemaker throughout life, coming to a firm resolution in a situation where friendship could be at risk felt strange and precarious. Deep within I called to God for guidance. The sky began to lighten, and with it there was a lifting of spirit. Then what happened next took me completely by surprise. Waves of bliss began to pour through me. I pulled into the car park to let off my daughter. The prospect of a half-hour wait did not bring on the usual sense of impatience. A presence, a wonderful presence, had captured my being, and all I could do was sit motionless, obedient to its beckoning. The surrounding buildings, the bare trees just in bud, and the passersby took on a new glow. It was as if the whole scene had been recharged with a light that shone from within and without, yet came from beyond.

11

From Rosalind's experience we can perhaps add one more quality to our list of characteristics of mystical hope. In some sense it is *atemporal*—that is, out of time. For some reason or another the experience pulls us out of the linear stream of hours and days ("the prospect of a half-hour wait did not bring on the usual sense of impatience") and imbues the moment we are actually in with an unexpected vividness and fullness. It is as if we had been transported, for the duration, into a wider field of presence, a direct encounter with Being itself. The poet T. S. Eliot talks about apprehending the "intersection of the timeless with time." These moments of mystical hope often bring with them an infusion of that timeless, expansive quality, jolting the ordered linearity of our lives into the immediacy of the now.

The spiritual life can only be lived in the present moment, in the now. All the great religious traditions insist upon this simple but difficult truth. When we go rushing ahead into the future or shrinking back into the past, we miss the hand of God, which can only touch us in the now. My favorite reminder on this point comes from the modern Sufi teacher Kabir Helminski: "Whoever makes all cares into one care, the care for simply being present, will be relieved of all care by that Presence, which is the creative power."[1] Obliquely but fully, these moments of mystical hope remind us of that Presence and reconnect us with it.

The Body of Hope

Many of you who have read my earlier book, *Love Is Stronger Than Death*,[2] will know something of my own immersion into the reality of this mystical hope. For five years I lived near and worked closely with a remarkable man and teacher, brother Raphael Robin, the hermit monk of St. Benedict's Monastery in Snowmass, Colorado. Toward the end of his life our close friendship became yet more intense when Rafe (as he was known by all) intuited during a time of intense solitary prayer that our partnership was intended to last "from here to eternity." He saw our relationship as headed straight through the walls of death, and he spent most of our remaining human time together helping me to be ready for this.

When he died of a heart attack early in Advent 1995, his body was brought home from the undertaker's to lie in wake in the monastery chapel for the entire night before the funeral mass. I spent the night there beside him, mostly by myself after the last monk gave up the vigil at 11 P.M. It was an experience of intense communion between us as the reality of the partnership Rafe had intuited slowly sank into every fiber of my being. But among the many mystical graces of that night, one of the most pungent came somewhere in the wee hours when I heard the words, in a voice distinctly Rafe's, "I'll meet you . . . in the body of hope."

14

The body of hope. What a strange, puzzling phrase! Neither one of us had ever used this expression in our physical lives. And yet the words were unmistakable, and I suspected that if I sat tight, I would soon find out what they meant.

I did. Not six weeks later, I happened to be strolling by the place I had lived in during those five years of working with Rafe—a rundown but still wonderfully funky and serviceable old ranch house—only to discover it being aggressively gutted by a new tenant. I had not been forewarned and, very new and tender in the grieving process, I was traumatized to see the remains of Rafe's handiwork on the place and the mementos of our life still stowed there unceremoniously dumped in a snowbank outside.

After the demolition derby had ended for the day, I sat down on the snowy deck of the old place and gave in to tears. Everything seemed hopeless. Rafe was gone, my life was gone, and now even the memories were being ripped apart.

And then the most extraordinary thing happened. As I sat out there shivering with cold and lost in my misery, suddenly, from my toes up, I could feel a strange lightness and joy start to bubble up in my being—almost like an empty glass being filled with champagne. It was not a mood shift, but a distinct physical sensation. There was an effervescence inside me that simply had not been there the moment before, as if I had been recharged, filled and fueled with an energy so light and buoyant that I simply could not sink even if I wanted to. Like Habakkuk, I found myself suddenly scooped up "on the heights," and soon even my feet were dancing.

Nothing had changed in the physical world. The Stanley place was still on the chopping block; what had been destroyed in the melee was still gone for good, and no force in heaven or earth was going to bring Rafe back into his physical body. And yet for the several minutes the experience lasted, none of this really mattered. I was above it all, my being coming to me from some far deeper place.

Grace?

But wouldn't it be simpler just to call these experiences moments of grace? For that is what they are, aren't they—times when God suddenly touches our lives with his blessing and renews us from the center of his own bottomless abundance?

Well, yes, that is quite true. Grace and mystical hope are close synonyms, and the outward effects are virtually identical. A person under the sway of grace and a person connected to the flow of mystical hope will display the same qualities of joy, gratitude, and a lightness and fullness of being even in the face of apparent reversal and defeat. Outwardly, they are dead ringers for each other, and even inwardly I believe they resonate with the same experience.

But words also have connotations, and this is why I make the distinction between grace and hope. For over the theological centuries calling an experience "grace"—such as Rosalind's in the car that afternoon—has come to connote something extraordinary and uncharacteristic: an infusion of divine sustenance into our lives as a special gift from God, given with God's own timing and discretion. Such a notion is consistent with the traditional theological viewpoint, where it seems that the first priority has always been to affirm the sovereign freedom of God and God's role as sole initiator. Using the term "grace" tends to lock us back into those traditional categories and allows us to go sailing right by the distinction I really want to highlight.

For in overemphasizing this divine freedom it is all too easy to understate and miss that hope is not intended to be an extraordinary infusion, *but an abiding state of being*. We lose sight of the invitation—and in fact, our *responsibility*, as stewards of creation—to develop a conscious and permanent connection to this wellspring. We miss the call to become a vessel, to become a chalice into which this divine energy can pour; a lamp through which it can shine.

But what if we are *intended* to become this vessel, this body of hope? What if, in fact, this effervescent, "lightness-of-being" energy is the fuel that drives our human life toward its divine fulfillment? What if our insistence on treating it as a rare and exceptional phenomenon is a way of ducking the invitation that was permanently extended at the Samarian well that blazing midday?

The journey to the wellspring, to the secret of Jesus, the Master of Galilee, is in fact the great inner journey to which we Christians are called. But like the sea voyage of the Celtic monk St. Brendan, on this journey we can reach our destination only if we learn to think and see in a new way.

In the medieval legend *The Voyage of St. Brendan,* Brendan sets out to search for the Land Promised to the Saints. But for seven years he keeps missing it—keeps sailing around in circles. He can find it only when something is reversed inside him. Instead of looking outward for landfalls and destinations, an inner eye opens within Brendan that can see the luminous fullness of the Land Promised to the Saints always and everywhere present beneath the surface motions of coming, going, striving, arriving. To find our way to that visionary world, that fullness at the heart of everything, as Rosalind did on a dreary January day in Victoria: this is the journey straight to the wellsprings of mystical hope. Come, are you ready to set out?

18

two

Living in the Mercy

*For as the heavens reach beyond earth
    and time,
we swim in mercy as in an endless sea.*

Psalm 103:11[1]

Before we can really begin to work with the idea of hope dwelling within rather than coming from without, we need to have some picture of where and how it could dwell in us, what inside us could embody it. Obviously there is a paradox here, an eye of the needle to thread. We ourselves are not the *source* of that hope; we do not manufacture it. But the source dwells deep within us and flows to us with an unstinting abundance, so much so that in fact it might be more accurate to say we dwell within *it*.

The story comes to mind of the little fish swimming up to its mother, all in a panic: "Mama, Mama, what's water? I gotta find water or I'll die!" We live immersed in this water, and the reason we miss it is not that it is so far away but, paradoxically, so close: more intimate to us than our being itself.

The term I will use to describe this embodying fullness is "the Mercy." It is the water in which we swim. Mercy is the length and breadth and height and depth of what we know of God—and the light by which we know it. You might even think of it as the Being of God insofar as we can possibly penetrate into it in this life, so that it is impossible to encounter God apart from the dimension of mercy.

The choice of term may seem a bit odd. Today "mercy"—along with so many of the other classic words in our spiritual tradition—has developed a negative connotation. It seems to suggest power and condescension, a transaction between two vastly unequal parties. A friend of mine, in fact, was told by her spiritual director that she should not pray the Jesus Prayer—"Lord Jesus Christ, have mercy on me," the mainstay of Eastern Orthodox contemplative spirituality—because "it reinforces medieval stereotypes of paternalism and powerlessness." Modern people, this spiritual director felt, need to be told that they are worthy, "that they can stand on their own two feet before God."

But the word "mercy" comes profoundly attested to in our Judeo-Christian spiritual heritage. Aside from the fact that the Jesus Prayer, hallowed by two millennia of Christian practice, has been consistently singled out by the spiritual masters of our path as *the* most powerful prayer a Christian can pray, we simply cannot get away from the Mercy without getting away from the

Bible as well. The word confronts us at every turn, as a living reality of our faith. It is all over the Old Testament, especially in the prophets and in the psalms. For a start, consider the following: "For I desire mercy, not sacrifice" (Hosea 6:6). "What does the LORD require of you? To act justly and to love mercy and to walk humbly with your God" (Micah 6:8). "He redeems your life from the grave and crowns you with mercy and loving-kindness" (Psalm 103:4). "He remembers his mercy and faithfulness to the house of Israel" (Psalm 98:4). "His mercy is everlasting" (Psalm 100:4). "His mercy endures forever" (Psalms 107:1 and 136:1). And while the frequency of references to mercy may decline somewhat in the New Testament, the quality of awareness surely does not—as evidenced, pointedly, in Jesus' parable of the Pharisee and the tax collector, which, even given our modern predilection for worthiness at all costs, must presumably pose something of a stumbling block to the spiritual director's summary dismissal of the Jesus Prayer.

In the Islamic tradition, growing out of those same Semitic roots, "mercy" is foremost among the names of God, and Islamic prayer begins always with the invocation, "In the name of God, the all merciful, the all compassionate...." One begins to suspect that this term "mercy" must have some pride of place that gets lost in the modern translations.

A Fierce, Bonding Love

Helen Luke, in her marvelous book *Old Age,* offers what may be the key to this riddle, discovered (of all places) in the *American Heritage Dictionary.* The word "mercy," she explains, derives from the ancient Etruscan word *merc*; the words "commerce" and "merchant" share this same root. And so at heart, mercy means some kind of exchange or transaction. It is a *connection* word. Elaborating on this somewhat surprising linguistic kinship, she explains:

> Like so many other meanings hidden in our language, the word commerce, debased to commercialism, has lost much of its dignity.... But the root meaning of exchange persisted and developed in another context, its meaning deepening through the French *merci* to grateful response and kindness of heart, and finally to the compassion and

forgiveness, including all our shades of darkness, whereby we are able to open ourselves to the Mercy. This is the ultimate "exchange" that, when we come to a final letting go, may reveal to us the whole.[2]

24   We are all "of the Mercy," Luke feels (and it is from her that I picked up my own preference for the term). Insofar as we are able to open our hearts and entrust ourselves to it, the Mercy is able to move us steadily toward that final letting go into the whole, which Luke describes elsewhere in her book through a striking image: "the weaving of the threads of life into the whole cloth of a shroud."[3] For Luke, the Mercy is first and foremost the great weaver, collecting and binding the scattered and broken parts of our lives in a tapestry of divine love.

Thomas Merton is thinking in a similar vein in his wonderful essay "The Good Samaritan." He points out that the word translated as "mercy" in English (*misericordia* in Latin) is *chesed* in the original Semitic, which actually means "a fierce, bonding love"—as between committed lovers. It is not about pity, but about passion. Merton writes: "*Chesed* [mercy] is fidelity, it is also strength. It is ultimate and unfailing because it is the power that binds one person to another, in a covenant of hearts."[4] So deep is this connection, Merton realizes, that even though the moods of God's anger may seem to come and go like passing clouds across the face of the sun, the Mercy itself—the sun—is unchanging, fundamental, and stable because "it is the love by which He seeks and chooses His chosen and binds them to himself."[5]

eternal changlessness

So when we think of mercy, we should be thinking first and foremost of a bond, an infallible link of love that holds the created and uncreated realms together. The mercy of God does not come and go, granted to some and refused to others. Why? Because it is unconditional—always there, underlying everything. It is literally the force that holds everything in existence, the gravitational field in which we live and move and have our being. Just like that little fish swimming desperately in search of water, we, too—in the words of Psalm 103—"swim in mercy as in an endless sea." Mercy is God's innermost being turned outward to sustain the visible and created world in unbreakable love.

To think this way perhaps takes some getting used to. From our traditional theological models we are used to thinking in terms of God "up there" and ourselves "down here"—God wholly unknown to us and of a fundamentally different substance, of which we are but a very distant reflection. But as the language of modern quantum physics penetrates increasingly into the basic metaphors of theology, allowing us to think more freely in terms of "conservation of energy," we can begin to see how God and creation actually exist in an energetic continuum. Just as we now know that matter is actually "condensed" energy (i.e., energy in a more dense and slow-moving form), would it be too great a leap to say that energy as we experience it—as movement, force, light—is a "condensation" of divine will and purpose? In other words, energy is what happens when divine Being expresses itself outwardly.

My daughter Lucy, in fact, stumbled quite innocently upon this insight at the tender age of three, when she came into my bedroom one morning singing a song she had made up:

I'll sing you a song of God in his heaven,
Where years turn to tables and trees
turn to love....

Years turn to tables: the subtle but palpable energy of time, measurable in our lives as the coherence of patterns and the weight of years, suddenly transformed itself in her child's imagination into something immediate and solid—a table. And in the same breath of her imagination, something equally immediate and solid, trees, "evaporated" into the more subtle but still palpable energy of love. Same God: different frequency, different outward manifestation. Einstein would have loved it.

So, too, would St. John the Evangelist. Lucy's insight certainly resonates profoundly with the opening lines of John's gospel:

In the beginning was the Word, and the Word was with God, and the Word was God. He was with God in the beginning. Through him all things were made; without him nothing was made that has been made.

(John 1:1-3)

27

If we understood Word to mean at root *vibration*—the outspeaking of the divine will and purpose—then the Word is that which makes manifest the fullness of divine purpose as it moves outward into form. This "energetic" reading of the gospel text might help explain the persistent mystical intuition undergirding so much of the New Testament that Jesus Christ, as the human incarnation of the divine Word (or *Logos*), is the fundamental ordering principle of the cosmos "in whom all things hold together."

One who has caught the profound theological implications of these developments in contemporary physics is the popular Episcopal preacher and writer Barbara Brown Taylor. Speaking of the "radical shift" in her image of God brought about by her exposure to quantum physics, she writes:

> Where is God in this picture? God is all over the place. God is up there, down here, inside my skin and out. God is the web, the energy, the space, the light—not captured in them, as if any of those concepts were more real than what unites them—but revealed in that singular, vast net of relationship that animates everything that is.[6]

From this remarkable insight, she moves on to an even more remarkable conclusion:

> At this point in my thinking, it is not enough for me to proclaim that God is responsible for all this unity. Instead, I want to proclaim that God *is* the unity— the very energy, the very intelligence, the very elegance and passion that make it all go.[7]

Her point may seem like a nuance, but it is a crucially important one. In other words—to express the implication of her insight in my own terms—our visible, created universe is not simply an object created by a wholly other God in order to manifest his love, but *that love itself*—the very heart of God, fully expressive in the dimension of time and form. Creation is not "somewhere else." A river runs through it. That river is God.

The Holy Element

When we speak in these terms, of course, we begin to use the classic language of the mystics, the language of visionary utterance. For seventeenth-century German visionary Jacob Boehme (a shoemaker by trade, whose voluminous cos-

mological treatises had their origin in a quarter of
an hour of intense mystical illumination) the
name in German for mercy was *Barmherzigkeit*—
"warmheartedness." Boehme saw mercy as "the
holy element": the root energy out of which all
else in the visible universe is made. The Mercy is
"holy substantiality"—the innermost essence of
being itself. It is that "river of God," running like
the sap through the tree of life.[8]

Lest we be inclined to discount this insight as
merely the rambling of a God-intoxicated
medieval mystic, it is astonishing to discover virtually an identical insight revealed by the contemporary and eminently sane psychotherapist
Gerald May, cofounder of the Shalem Institute for
Spiritual Direction in Bethesda, Maryland. In a
striking chapter in his book *Will and Spirit,* May
affirms that from a clinical standpoint, once the
various differentiations and feeling-tones have
been stripped away from our subjective emotional life, what remains is a raw, root energy that is,
finally, none other than divine love. "It is as if
agape [divine love] were the base metal, irreducible and unadulterated," he writes. "The uni-

verse runs on an energy that is, at its core, unconditionally loving."[9]

May's vision of *agape*—divine love—is very
close to Boehme's (and my own) notion of the
Mercy. Far from pity or condescension, it is the
very heartbeat of God resonant in creation; the
warmth that pulses through all things as the
divine Mystery flows out into created form.

31

Mercy and Hope

If you have stayed with my argument so far, even
in a willing-suspension-of-disbelief sort of way,
you will find yourself suddenly set down in a very
different universe from the one we have grown
accustomed to inhabiting in these recent, post-
Enlightenment centuries. Rather than living in a
"clockwork" universe run on implacable scientif-
ic principles by an absentee landlord God—or,
even more desolate, a totally random, nobody-in-
charge universe where the only law is the law of
the jungle—instead you wake up inside a warm-
hearted and purposive intelligence, a coherence of
which you yourself are part of the expression.

This is the world of the Mercy. And it is, in
fact, the world of all ancient and perennial religious consciousness, for which quantum physics

is merely the latest purveyor of a wisdom supplied in former days by visionary imagination. The Greek patristic fathers, who were well acquainted with this world, called it "the intelligible universe," of which our own "sensible universe" is a cross-section in time and space. More recently, the modern Sufi master Kabir Helminski speaks of this inner, engendering, and sustaining universe as "the electromagnetic field of love."[10]

Now it was this intelligible universe that my own teacher Rafe came to know and move about in toward the end of his life, and what I believe he was insisting on when he named it "the *body* of hope." Our continuing journey together beyond his physical death would not be simply a matter of sporadic mystical visitations seemingly in defiance of the laws of nature, but would unfold within a coherent field, obeying its own laws of higher causality. This field is like a "luminous web" (as Barbara Brown Taylor calls it), intended to connect and interweave everything, in which all the knot ends of reality come together in a huge tapestry of divine love. To see it is like suddenly being able to see the love itself, the pattern in the random dots of the universe.

To say that this body of hope is really an energy field may be confusing, I realize, to readers accustomed to thinking of a body as a solid, corpuscular thing. But practitioners of Asian medicine, along with the quantum physicists, have also long shared this belief, considering the outer, or physical, body to be interpenetrated by more subtle, energetic bodies: the etheric, astral, and causal, to be specific. (The causal body correlates closely with what the Greek patristic fathers called "the intelligible.") And innumerable mystics, both eastern and western, have spoken of the experience, generally accessed in states of *samahdi* (deep contemplative prayer), of encountering their own body in exactly the way Barbara Brown Taylor describes: as a luminous web. In the language of both quantum physics and perennial mysticism, "body" is simply another word for an organized energy field, irrespective of its physical density.

But is it really there, this body of hope? For the time being, all I would ask of you is a continued (willing suspension of disbelief.) If it could be shown to be true that our life is connected to an innermost essence of great profundity and power, and that access to it is through what is innermost in our own selves, then we would have not only a conceptual understanding of mystical hope, but a practical way of orienting ourselves toward it. Mystical hope would simply be what happens when we touch this innermost ground and it floods forth into our being as strength and joy. Hope would be the Mercy—divine love itself—coursing through our being like lightning finding a clear path to the ground.

The Point Vierge

If we dwell in the Mercy, does it also dwell in us? If mercy is about a connection, then presumably there must be an actual point of contact where our own innermost ground and the Mercy meet as simply One.

For centuries Christian mystics have spoken about that point of interface, but in language veiled and hedged, since it is a primary requirement of Christian theological orthodoxy that the distinction between creator and creature—between God and ourselves—be stringently preserved. But visionary insight (and certainly this can be verified through personal experience as we converge toward our own center) reveals that as

34

we so converge, the membrane between the worlds gets thinner and thinner; the sense of intertwining is more and more mysterious. Where does God "end" and "I" begin? Even the phrasing of the question reveals its essential speciousness.

"There is in the soul a something in which God dwells, and there is in the soul a something in which the soul dwells in God," writes Meister Eckhart—cautiously picking his way around the words.[11] This mysterious *something* Eckhart calls "the foundation of the soul." It has been described over and over—the "inner light" of Quaker mystic George Fox, for example—but perhaps nowhere more clearly and eloquently than in Thomas Merton's remarkable essay "A Member of the Human Race." Here Merton recalls his own initiation into the same kind of unitive seeing my friend Rosalind described earlier:

> In Louisville, at the corner of 4th and Walnut, in the middle of the shopping district, I was suddenly overwhelmed by the realization that I loved all these people, that they were mine and I was theirs.... [12]

35

For a moment his illusory sense of separateness melted and he was at one, in the heart of God, with the whole of humanity. Pondering the source of this unity, Merton concludes the essay in a burst of pure visionary splendor:

36

Again, that expression, *le point vierge* (I cannot translate it) comes in here. At the center of our being is a point of nothingness which is untouched by sin and illusion, a point of pure truth, a point or spark which belongs entirely to God, which is never at our disposal, from which God disposes of our lives, which is inaccessible to the fantasies of our own mind or the brutalities of our own will. This little point of nothingness and of absolute poverty is the pure glory of God written in us, as our poverty, as our indigence, as our sonship. It is like a pure diamond blazing with the invisible light of heaven. It is in everybody, and if we could see it, we would see these billions of points of light coming together in the face and blaze of a sun that would make all the darkness and cruelty of life vanish completely. I have no program for

this seeing. It is only given. But the gate of
heaven is everywhere.[13]

While Merton claims not to be able to translate this phrase *le point vierge* ("the virgin
point"), he in fact does so clearly in several of his
other writings. The term itself he picked up from
the French scholar Louis Massignon, who in turn
was translating ninth-century Sufi mystic Al
Hallaj's treatise on the heart. The *point vierge* is
the "last, irreducible, secret center of the heart
where God alone penetrates"; where the last veils
of our createdness give way into God's all-enfold-
ing mercy. In an earlier passage in *Conjectures of
a Guilty Bystander* Merton had noted:

> Massignon has some deeply moving pages
> in the *Mardis de Dar-es-Salam*: about the
> desert, the tears of Agar [Hagar], the
> Muslims, the "point vierge" of the spirit,
> the center of our nothingness where, in
> apparent despair, one meets God—and is
> found completely in His mercy.[14]

Merton's writing in these passages is both bold
and cautious. Bold in that he claims—perhaps
more clearly than any other Christian mystical

writer to my knowledge—that at the center of our being is an innermost point of truth which shares not only the likeness, but even the *substance* of God's own being. And yet cautious in that, following the bent of Christian tradition, Merton makes it clear that access to this center is not at our command. *We* cannot get to it; it can only get to us by flowing from the innermost outward into our being. Furthermore, he is even more insistent than his Sufi sources that this flow is entered only through our complete poverty—our complete nothingness. Joining a long stream of mystics, he insists that what is true being appears in this realm as non-being, as nothingness, and can be approached only through a way of being that, in our ordinary consciousness, seems totally counter-instinctive: a way of being that embraces poverty, unknowing, surrender, death. We cannot find this innermost, but only *be found* by it in our wholehearted willingness to join it at the point of nothing. This is the koan that dissolves the illusory dichotomy between grace and works, and allows that access point—which we know in our hearts is truly there—to draw us into the luminous web. It is through this little point or spark of

38

loose your life to find it

pure truth that the Mercy flows into us and through us. It is the spring at the bottom of the well of our being through which hope is continually renewed.

Merton's experience of the *point vierge* did not grow out of reading about Sufism. It grew from his own deep experience of contemplative prayer, where one swims down into the depths and finds, at the wellspring of one's being, the "hidden ground of love," as Merton calls it. As a teacher of contemplative prayer myself, I find over and over that those who are drawn to this path are drawn to the innermost—which they realize is not personal divinized selfhood, but the divine ground itself, manifesting in and through their individual form. In workshop after workshop I meet people (many of them no longer practicing Christians) who despite all theological indoctrination about the complete otherness of God have stood their ground, firm in their innate knowledge that at the foundation of the soul, at that *point vierge,* something of our being presses deep into the heart of God and begins to swim in the infinite ocean of God's mercy. That ocean is our source and substance, the ground of our own arising, the foundation of hope. Those who experience it may leave the church, but they do not leave this ground. Once experienced, it is undeniable.

three

Meditation and Hope

The notion that God is absent is the fundamental illusion of the human condition.

Thomas Keating

At this point, then, we need to talk more about contemplative prayer, or *meditation,* to use its generic name. In the last chapter we saw how the journey to the wellsprings of hope is really a journey toward the center, toward the innermost ground of our being where we meet and are met by God. But when we speak about a journey to our innermost center, it is almost impossible to avoid speaking about meditation.

Well, perhaps not *quite* impossible. Bede Griffiths, one of the great contemplative masters of our time, claimed that there are actually three routes to the center. You can have a near-death experience. You can fall desperately in love. Or you can begin a practice of meditation. Of the three, he said with a somewhat mischievous smile, meditation is probably the most reliable starting point.

For more than a decade now I have been a teacher of centering prayer, a simple form of Christian meditational prayer developed and popularized by Thomas Keating, a Trappist monk and former abbot, now resident at St. Benedict's Monastery in Snowmass, Colorado.[1] Centering prayer teaches a basic, no-nonsense method of

42

self-emptying—simply letting go of thoughts as they arise—to help practitioners break out of their compulsive attachment to thinking and entrust themselves to the deeper stillness of God.

Whether by centering prayer or some other method, I consider meditation a fundamental starting point for Christian understanding and practice. Why? Because meditation, more than any other spiritual practice, nurtures the latent capacities within us that can perceive and respond to divine hope. In the classic language of our tradition, these capacities are known as the "spiritual senses."

If I am right in what I was saying earlier, then the Mercy is always with us; it is the ground and wellspring of our being. But unless we can connect with it, we miss the whole show—and we do not really understand the "good news" that our gospel is founded upon. It is possible to be swimming in a sea of mercy and still experience ourselves as stranded on shore. This distorted perception is what meditation is intended to fix.

Egoic Thinking

In the first chapter we spoke about how in our usual sense of things hope is tied to outcome. This

43

means that it is pinned on something outside of ourselves, such as a new job or a new relationship, and we look outside of ourselves to find it. Another way of expressing this same idea would be to say that our usual sense of hope is tied to an "egoic" way of thinking, because "looking outside of itself" is exactly the process by which the ego thinks.

44

When I use the term "egoic thinking," I am not trying to make a value judgment. I am not talking about selfishness or "sinful self will"—at least not yet. I am simply talking about the biochemistry of the mind; how our mental apparatus is set up. As human beings we are gifted with what is known as "self-reflexive consciousness": the capacity to stand outside ourselves and look upon ourselves in third person. As far as we know, we are the only species so gifted. Because of this unique capacity of the mind, we are able to experience ourselves as distinct persons, made up of distinct qualities, capacities, and needs: "I am a person who likes the ocean." "I have a quick temper." "I am a cat-person...a dog-person...an introvert...a person who needs order in her life." Through this same gift, we are able to project ourselves back into the past or forward into the future: remembering, planning, visioning. We can dream of different realities and set them in motion. This is the great endowment of the human mind and the reason for our extraordinary evolutionary success. It is why we see ourselves (rightly or wrongly) as the stewards of creation and not simply mechanical parts within it.

45

But there is a downside to this same self-reflexive capacity. Built into the texture of egoic thinking is the tendency to experience one's personal identity as separate—composed of distinct qualities, defined by what holds one apart from the whole. And because of this double-edged sword, the ego is chronically anxious. It simply cannot get "enough"—enough praise, enough security, enough accomplishment—to overcome that dreadful sense of being separate and separated, of having secretly failed at the mission of bringing the "self" into fullness.

Again, this is simply part of the biochemistry of egoic thinking. But you can see how quickly "sinful self will" springs up in this seedbed of anxiety. When I experience myself as separate from everyone else, it creates an automatic mentality of scarcity and an automatic sense of competing for limited resources. Another person's gain is at least potentially my loss, so I need to be constantly vigilant that my rights and needs are being upheld; that I am not being taken advantage of. This, of course, is the entire point of Jesus' parable of the laborers in the vineyard, where the foreman pays everyone the same wage whether they have worked for twelve hours or for one. It is a devastating satire of that way of thinking—the compulsive need to keep track of more and less. The catch is that, just like a Zen koan, as long as you are in egoic consciousness, you will not get it.

Fortunately, though—and this is the point that spiritual masters of all traditions have made since time immemorial—this is not the way things really are. The sense of scarcity and threat is a distorted perception simply created by the egoic way of thinking, in the same way that a lens under water will refract a ray of incoming light, making it appear to be a bent line. If you are feeling worried, frantic, slighted, or wounded, you may or may not have an actual problem. (It is amazing how often those perceptions coming from negative feelings prove to be inaccurate!) But one thing *is* sure, and that is that you are in the egoic mode of thinking—for that is the level at which all these feelings arise, and in which they are contained.

This statement may sound too categorical and in need of nuancing. But all great spiritual teachers—including our own Anointed One in his beautiful teachings on the lilies of the field—have insisted upon it, and invited people to "check it out" in their own experience. To get out of the turmoil, according to spiritual teaching, you actually have two options. You can either stay in the egoic perception and try to deal with the problem at that level—or you can shift to a whole new way of perceiving.

47

Ordinary and Spiritual Awareness

You may have noticed that those three experiences Bede Griffiths mentioned as "pathways to the center" have one thing in common: they all catapult us out of ego-centered consciousness. Those who come back from a near-death experience bring with them a visceral remembrance of how vivid and abundant life is when the sense of separateness has dropped away. Those who fall profoundly in love experience a dying into the other that melts every shred of their own identity, self-definition, caution, and boundaries, until finally there is no "I" anymore—only "you." Those who meditate go down to the same place, but by a back staircase deep within their own being.

48

Deeper than our sense of separateness and isolation is another level of awareness in us, another whole way of knowing. Thomas Keating, in his teachings on centering prayer, calls this our "spiritual awareness" and contrasts it with the "ordinary awareness" of our usual, egoic thinking. The simplest way of describing this other kind of awareness is that while the self-reflexive ego thinks by means of noting differences and drawing distinctions, spiritual awareness "thinks" by an innate perception of kinship, of belonging to the whole.

Celts

I realize that this way of talking is not easy to understand. It goes against the very grain of our language (which mirrors our usual thinking processes) and thus skitters off into the realm of poetry and mystical utterance. The Christian contemplative tradition abounds with descriptions of the "spiritual senses"—these more subtle faculties of intuitive perception—but in language that is often so allegorical and dense it obscures more than it reveals. Let me see if I can describe this same thing in a simpler way, in terms of an experience I came to know only too well during my years in Maine: sailing in the fog.

On a bright, sunny day you can set your course on a landfall five miles away from you and sail right to it. But in the fog, you make your way by paying close attention to all the things immediately around you: the deep roll of the sea swells as you enter open ocean, the pungent scent of spruce boughs, or the livelier tempo of the waves as you approach the land. You find your way by being sensitively and sensuously connected to exactly where you are, by letting "here" reach out and lead you. You will not learn that in the navigation courses, of course. But it is part of the local knowledge that all the fishermen and natives use to steer by. You know you belong to a place when you can find your way home by feel.

All in all, this little metaphor is a pretty good analogy of how these two levels of awareness actually work. If egoic thinking is like sailing by reference to where you are not—by what is out there and up ahead—spiritual awareness is like sailing by reference to where you *are*. It is a way of "thinking" at a much more visceral level of yourself—responding to subtle intimations of presence too delicate to pick up at your normal level of awareness, but which emerge like a sea swell from the ground of your being once you relax and allow yourself to belong deeply to the picture.

[handwritten margin note: Being present]

Because of this visceral dimension, some writers speak of spiritual awareness in terms of the heart being "magnetized" to God, responding to a magnetic pull from the center just as the compass needle points to magnetic north. And the center, of course, is the *point vierge*.

In Thomas Keating's diagram of the "levels of awareness," which consists of three concentric circles like a hunting target, he places inside the spiritual awareness circle, like the bullseye of the target, something he calls "the divine awareness." I was there once when a student asked him, "Is that your own most intimate awareness of God, or is God himself actually being aware *through* you?" To which Fr. Keating merely smiled and said, "Well, that will give you something to ponder!" Clearly, they were both circling around that same mysterious terrain of the innermost described so profoundly by Thomas Merton.

The point is that our spiritual awareness seems to be given to us in order to hone in on and not lose touch with that "point or spark of pure truth" at the core of our being, from which both the true compass track of our life and our existential conviction of belonging emanate. That is what the magnetic pull is all about. And as we learn gradually to trust it and let it draw us along, we discover that those core fears of the egoic level—that something terrible can happen to us, that we can fall out of God or suffer irreparable harm—do not compute in these deeper waters of our being. Try as we will, we simply cannot find them there. They can only affect us when we are at the surface of ourselves.

True Metanoia

Almost nobody *chooses* to go sailing in the fog. You have to be forced out of the nest. And it is pretty much the same with meditation. As long as we can get by using our old way of thinking, most of us will—and so this other, deeper way of knowing remains largely latent within us. Not until we are slammed against the wall, when the yearning for truth becomes overwhelming in us and we have the sense that everything done in the ordinary way of consciousness merely ends in lies and disillusionment, do we consent to leave the familiar waters of egoic navigation.

But when that moment arrives, you might think of meditation as a kind of wager you make with yourself. The wager is this: that this other way of thinking actually exists in you, this level that knows how to sail in the fog, see in the dark. (And why do you suppose the great contemplative masters of our tradition give their works such titles as *The Cloud of Unknowing,* or the *Dark Night of the Soul?*) The only thing blocking the emergence of this whole and wondrous other way of knowing is your over-reliance on your ordinary thinking. If you can just turn that off for a while, then the other will begin to take shape in you, become a reality you can actually experience. And as it does, you will know, in a way you cannot presently know, your absolute belonging and place in the heart of God, and that you are a part of this heart forever and cannot possibly fall out of it, no matter what may happen.

That is the wager. Meditation, then, becomes a way of screening out the noise, turning down the boom box of your egoic thinking to allow this other to begin to resonate within you. Thomas Keating speaks of it humorously as "taking a small vacation from yourself." Whatever form of meditation you practice, it is in essence simply a method for detaching yourself from thinking (which tends to reinforce the egoic process) long enough for you to begin to trust this other, deeper intelligence moving inside you. It provides you with another way to think: from "beyond the mind"—which, incidentally, is what the word *metanoia*, usually translated as "repentance," actually means.

Centering Prayer and Meditation

The reclaiming of meditation as a core discipline of the Christian path is one of the most significant spiritual developments of our times. There are now tens of thousands of Christians worldwide practicing meditation daily, the majority of them using either centering prayer or Christian meditation (a parallel discipline developed by the late Dom John Main). In the Christian east, of course, meditation never dropped out of sight; the Jesus

Prayer, which in both form and substance is a classic Christian mantra, has always been a mainstay of Orthodox spirituality.

But of the various forms of meditation now widely available to Christian practitioners, I continue to gravitate to centering prayer as the one most uniquely congruent with both the theology and the underlying temperament of Christianity because of a particular slant of its teaching. Other forms of meditation may emphasize stilling the mind or developing single-pointed concentration. But in centering prayer the whole emphasis is on consent—or surrender—"to the presence and action of God," as Thomas Keating puts it.

Unlike other forms of meditation which prescribe the continuous repetition of a prayer word, or mantra, the teaching in centering prayer is simply, "Sit in the presence of God. And whenever you notice you are thinking, just let the thought go." Not because thinking is bad, but because the goal is to maintain a space of deep inner availability to God—deeper than thoughts, deeper than emotions—and the thinking gets in the way. A "sacred word" is used to help facilitate this prompt release of thoughts, but unlike a mantra it

letting go into the Presence

is used only sporadically, not as a continuous touchstone for the attention.

This subtle difference in emphasis is beautifully illustrated in one of the classic centering prayer teaching stories. A nun, after her first try at centering prayer during a workshop led by Thomas Keating, came up to him in great frustration. "I'm such a failure at this prayer," she said. "In twenty minutes of sitting I've had ten thousand thoughts."

"How lovely," Fr. Keating responded, without so much as batting an eye. "Ten thousand opportunities to return to God!"

And that is the essence of centering prayer. The "magic" of this prayer is not attained by keeping the mind perfectly still or clear. It happens in each moment you catch yourself thinking and are willing to let that thought go as a symbol of your consent to open up fully, let go of your own stuff, and simply hold a space of total availability given to God as a free gift of your love for the duration of the prayer period.

"Not my will but thine be done, O Lord"— over and over, thought by thought, ten-thousand-thoughts by ten-thousand-thoughts. I call it "boot camp in Gethsemani" because in this simple form of meditation we are practicing that core gesture of the Christian faith: total surrender of ourselves into the hands of God. And so, yes, we are doing what all meditation does—putting a stick in the spokes of egoic thinking and allowing a new way of knowing to emerge in us. But when we do these things within the context of centering prayer, this emergence has a distinct warm-heartedness to it, a *Barmherzigkeit* (to pick up on an important tip-off from Jacob Boehme) that is the characteristic flavor of centering prayer, clearly recognizable to all who work with this prayer, particularly in groups. While this warmth is sometimes disconcerting to those used to more austere disciplines of meditation, there is a reason for its presence. Centering prayer, with its emphasis not on clarity of the mind but on surrender of the heart, leads straight down into the heart's depths, straight toward the *point vierge*. It becomes a direct encounter with the Mercy.

four

Dying Before You Die

In the middle of winter I discovered in myself an invincible summer.

Albert Camus

I was first introduced to this quotation from Camus in the form of a poster that hung next to the bedside of my mother as she died of cancer. What it meant to her I cannot say; she was well beyond explaining herself. But the poster came to me as her express bequest, and it has been a faithful benchmark in my own journey toward the wellsprings of mystical hope.

What I want to talk about in this chapter is that hard ground—those situations in which there appears to be no hope, no way out. And here, it seems that our Christian faith is uniquely vulnerable. Because we are a resurrection faith, because one of the core images of the gospels is Jesus the healer asking us to believe that "all things are possible," we assume too often that our faith—if only we have enough—can fix anything. So in those situations where the fixing does not occur, the pain of loss is often aggravated by a deep sense of abandonment and disillusionment. As a pastor, I deal daily with the wreckage of those whose faith died with a loved one. Many Buddhist and other spiritual masters specifically castigate Christianity on this point, insisting that only when we move *beyond* hope is there any possibility of healing. Hope will always take us outside of ourselves into want and need, back into the illusion of separateness that is the only real problem in the first place.

But of course they are talking about the usual hope, the surface hope. The *ground* of hope is very real and immensely powerful—if you have the courage to yield yourself all the way into it. The real problem with much of our Christian presentation of hope and healing is that it does not push far enough: it stays at the fix-it level. Beneath that is something infinitely deeper and truer.

In the last chapter I talked about meditation as the key to learning to think in a new way. But the real point of meditation is not to reject all ideas and concepts; Christianity does not say that the way to end pain is to end thinking. What it says, rather, is that we have to get beyond linear, discursive thinking in order to access the realm of inspired visionary knowing where Christianity finally becomes fully congruent with its own highest truth, and its mystical treasures can be received into an awakened heart. This deeper way of thinking has been called in our tradition the "unitive," and awakening it has long been the goal of the Christian monastic practice known as *lectio divina,* or "sacred reading" of the scripture.[1] Unitive thinking is more like poetry than systematic theology, and it relies on the participation of the unconscious (which is what meditation helps free up). Here at this level lie the ideas that can really help us to get a handle on the "width and length and height and depth" of mystical hope, and why it can never ultimately fail us.

In this chapter, then, with the help of poetry and drama, I want to try to swim down into some of these deeper waters.

The Fullness of Time

In the well-loved film *Babette's Feast,* adapted from a tale by Isak Dinesen, we are plunged into an extraordinary tale of love and loss. By a series of coincidences, a woman named Babette, a former *cordon bleu* chef in Paris who lost everything in the terrorist uprisings of 1871, flees to Denmark and is taken in by two aging sisters who have dedicated their entire lives to religious work. It turns out that they, too, have lost much in order to serve their little spiritual flock, each having given up the man of her dreams and the opportunity for fame and fortune. Now, years later, they are weary and disillusioned, their community aging and bickering among themselves, things drifting toward disintegration. In a sudden plot twist Babette learns that she has won the lottery back in Paris and decides to use the entire proceeds—10,000 francs—to give a banquet for all of them. Stunned, these Danish peasants sit in gradually mellowing bewonderment as course after course of gourmet French cooking (each with its own proper wine, crystal goblets, china, and flatware) is set before them.

There is a special guest at the table that evening: General Lowenhielm, the man who years before had sought the hand of one of the sisters. Now, briefly reunited with the woman he has always loved though time wrenched them to a separate destiny, he rises and offers a toast:

"Mercy and truth have met together. Righteousness and bliss shall kiss one another," he begins, quoting a verse from Psalm 85. Then, in what becomes the film's eloquent climax, he continues:

Man in his weakness and shortsightedness believes he must make choices in this life.

He trembles at the risk he takes. We do know fear. But no. Our choice is of no importance. There comes a time when our eyes are opened. And we come to realize that mercy is infinite. We need only await it with confidence and receive it with gratitude. Mercy imposes no conditions.

And, lo! Everything we have chosen has been granted to us. And everything we rejected has also been granted. Yes, we get back even what we rejected. For mercy and truth are met together. Righteousness and bliss shall kiss one another.[2]

So much of that hopelessness of our lives, it seems, comes from the inevitable sense of time running out, of things being taken away. After all, there is only one course through time. As we age, the accumulation of regret for the many roads not taken, the choices we made that have made other choices impossible—even, sometimes, the sense of having made a decisive wrong turn and wasted the one chance we were given—begins to weigh heavily upon us. Like General Lowenhielm, we find ourselves far downstream of our life's true course, caught in the tangle of our own cumulative bad decisions with no way to extricate ourselves.

Or is there? This brings us to one of the most wondrous aspects of the Mercy that the General, with the eyes of his heart wide open, instinctively recognizes. Theologians sometimes speak of this aspect as the *apocatastasis,* the final restoration of all things "at the end of time."

I first wrapped my mind around this concept by way of a strong visual image that came to me one Sunday many years ago when I was still living in Maine. I had put my daughter Lucy, by then a teenager, on a ferry from our island to the mainland four miles away to meet her boyfriend Scott. Standing on a high bluff on an exceptionally clear afternoon, I could watch the whole little drama play out. I saw each of the sequences unfolding in turn: the ferry approaching the dock, Scott's car winding down the landing road, Lucy moving to the front of the boat in eager expectation. I could feel their excitement about the rendezvous that was finally almost upon them. But from my vantage point, it was all present already, all contained in a huge, stately "now." The dimension that for them was still being lived in time, for me had been converted to space, and the picture was complete.

I grasped that day what *apocatastasis* really means, a concept that had eluded me for years. I saw how time—all our times—are contained in something bigger: a space that is none other than the Mercy itself. The fullness (or "end") of time becomes this space: a vast, gentle wideness in which all possible outcomes—all our little histories, past, present, and future; all our hopes and dreams—are already contained and, mysteriously, *already fulfilled.*

The great mystics have named this as the heart of the Mercy of God: the intuition that the entire rainbow of times and colors, of past and future, of individual paths through history, is all contained—flows out of and back into—that great white light of the simple loving presence of God. *Alpha* and *Omega,* beginning and end. And in that Mercy all our history—our possible pasts and possible futures, our lost loved ones and children never born—is contained and fulfilled in a wholeness of love from which nothing can ever possibly be lost.

It is not a vision we can stand too long in the presence of. General Lowenhielm knew it briefly at the banquet table that evening. So, too, did the contemporary poet Dylan Thomas in a little known poem called "This Side of the Truth" that is nonetheless among his finest. Dedicated to the poet's six-year-old son, Llewellyn, the poem beautifully elucidates how all those apparently irreconcilable opposites of our lives—innocence and guilt, success and failure, triumph and loss—are somehow encompassed in a deeper, unifying forgiveness. In the end, Thomas affirms, neither good nor bad has the final word, but

> all your deeds and words,
> Each truth, each lie,
> Die in unjudging love.[3]

If only we could understand this more deeply! If only we could see and trust that all our ways of getting there, all our courses over time—our good deeds, our evil deeds, our regrets, our compulsive choosings and the fallout from those choosings, our things left undone and paths never actualized—are quietly held in an exquisite fullness that simply poises in itself, then pours itself out in a single glance of the heart. If we could only glimpse that, even for an instant, then perhaps we would be able to sense the immensity of the love that seeks to meet us at the crossroads of the Now, when we yield ourselves entirely into it.

My teacher Rafe was strongly convinced that he could work with his parents, both long dead, to help release them from the pain of issues still unresolved during their earthly lives—his father's alcoholism and suicide, his mother's bitterness— simply by encountering them in the Mercy, at the white hot point of that "unjudging love." It was a profound work, with considerable healing for himself as well. Toward the end of his life he became increasingly certain that things done or left undone in life are merely a tiny tip of the iceberg that represents the actual reality of our being. By surrendering to the Mercy at the innermost point of his own being, Rafe was convinced that he would enter that causal "ground zero" from which his life could continuously re-create itself in love—even after his physical death. Because of this, he accepted with complete serenity that the parts of our human walk we did not get to live out together because of his monastic vows and the age difference between us—"the road not taken" of marriage and raising a family—were already completely contained in the quality of the love between us in each moment. If I could simply learn to lean into the fullness of this love, its own bright causality would continue to light the path of my unfolding. Not by mourning for him, not by copying his life from the outside, but simply by rejoining him over and again at that innermost point of the Mercy our life not lived in time would re-create itself in love.

Rafe was a hermit and a mystic. Yet not long ago I saw essentially the same insight conveyed with brilliant firmness by my friend Jamien back in Maine who died after a ten-year struggle with breast cancer, but not before raising her four sons to a point where she knew they would be able to understand her final instructions. Sixteen-year-old Sam writes:

> Before she lost her voice, she called all her boys around her and told us to keep our eyes open after she died, because although she would be gone from her body, she said she would still exist in smaller things, and she hoped we would recognize them.

Although these smaller things don't always jump out at me, when they come back to mind, I realize she was right....she is there. Jamien Morehouse is someone who will never leave my life, and that is truly wonderful.

Jamien's greatest gift to her sons was the insistence that they did not need to lead their lives looking backward. Rather, by keeping their eyes and hearts open, they would encounter her always afresh as the current of her love for them carried them buoyantly toward their futures. This is the first great mystery of the Mercy.

Dying Before You Die

And yet we struggle against that knowing, struggle for all we are worth. Some say that the great tragedy of human life is that we struggle so hard against that which, once yielded into, becomes the immediate fulfillment of all we have longed for.

In Tolstoy's great novella *The Death of Ivan Ilych*, he describes how Ivan, down to the final days of his life, screaming and struggling against going into what he perceives to be the "black sack" of his death, suddenly experiences a shift like the sensation one sometimes experiences in a railway carriage when one thinks one is going backward while one is really going forward and suddenly becomes aware of the real direction.... In place of death there was light. "So that's what it is!" he suddenly exclaimed aloud. "What joy!"[4]

69

To a few of the truly spiritually courageous it has seemed, then, that the real trick would be to end the resistance—go through that inner shift of direction—*before* the end of one's actual physical life. The practice is called "dying before you die," and it represents the highest aspiration of all the spiritual paths. "For the mystery of 'Die before you die' is this," explains the great Sufi poet Jallaludin Rumi: "that the gifts come after you die and not before."[5] Only after the terror of one's own diminishment and annihilation, after the last scraps of clinging to life at any cost have been left behind forever, is it possible to truly live in hope.

Thomas Merton speaks of this practice in an astonishing lecture "True Freedom," given to the novices at Gethsemani abbey not long before his own death. He begins by commenting on a text by the poet Rilke that describes a visit to that same Russia of Tolstoy's novels: "The Russians do not conceive of God as a mightily enthroned power who lifts up man's burdens, but rather as a protecting nearness that does not permit final destruction."

70

"So when do you get to know this God for real?" Merton asks the novices, then answers his own question:

> God is near to us at the point that is just before final destruction. Take away everything else down to that point of final destruction, and the last little bit that's left before destruction, a little kernel of gold which is the essence of you—and there is God protecting it. . . . And this is something terrific.
>
> The real freedom is the freedom to be able to come and go from that center, and to be able to do without anything that is not immediately connected to that center. Because when you die, that is all that is left. When we die, everything is destroyed except this one thing, which is our reality and

which is the reality that God preserves forever. He will not permit its final destruction.

And the thing is, that we know this. This is built into that particular little grain of gold, this spark of the soul or whatever it is. It *knows* this. And the freedom that matters is the capacity to be in contact with that center. Because it is from that center that everything comes.... [But] we don't normally get into that center unless we're brought to the edge of what looks like destruction. In other words, we have to be facing the possibility of the destruction of everything else to know *this* will not be destroyed.[6]

71

Most of us are not ready to take it this far. And fortunately, most of us are not asked to jump into the spiritual journey just before that point of final destruction. It is all right to work ourselves toward it gradually, and meditation offers a wonderful way to do just that. Because it puts us immediately in touch with that "little kernel of gold which is the essence of you" and allows us to begin to recognize it and trust it, meditation essentially simulates that knowing which Merton says is usually gained only at the point of final destruction: the knowing that "*this* will not be destroyed." This gradual learning is accelerated in a practice such as centering prayer because of its emphasis on the surrender of the heart, which also precisely replicates the *process* by which this inner knowing is ultimately released.

But as we work our way gradually toward that final release, it is comforting to know that some have sought out that place deliberately, pushing through their own fear and resistance to break forth into that sacred ground where mystical hope becomes a living reality. Those saints like Julian of Norwich who have lain near death and recovered, or those like Thérèse of Lisieux who have teetered on that same brink and passed across, and still others like Etty Hillesum, that remarkable young Jewish woman who in the midst of a concentration camp discovered in herself the wellsprings of inexhaustible compassion and joy—all these bold-spirited adventurers tease us away from any notion that hope will fail us. Only if we are still hanging on, they remind us; only in the measure that we fail to yield completely into the mercy of God, will hope fail us. If we are willing to take it all the way, it will take us all the way. This is the second great Mystery of the Mercy.

The Body of Christ

Ultimately, this is the journey that even Jesus had to take. At the moment of his arrest, according to Matthew's gospel, as one of the disciples scurries to defend his master, Jesus orders, "Put your sword back in its place.... Do you think I cannot call on my Father, and he will at once put at my disposal more than twelve legions of angels?" (Matthew 26:52-53). But the story stipulates clearly that Jesus, like all the rest of us, must pass through the ground of his own powerlessness and hopelessness. There is to be no hope in the usual sense, no mightily enthroned power to lift up his burdens. He, too, must discover that "protecting nearness" in his own innermost ground.

Christian tradition has always intuited—though not always for reasons fully clear—that it was this yielding into the ground that was essential to the act of salvation: Christ's *death* rather than simply his resurrection. The passage through final destruction had to be made, for in it—and

73

only in it—a corner was turned that became the cornerstone of our salvation.

What could this corner be? My sense is that it has something to do with that same psalm verse General Lowenhielm quoted: "Mercy and truth have met together; righteousness and bliss have kissed each other"—or as it has been more recently translated, "Mercy and faithfulness have met; justice and peace have embraced." When Jesus, the living truth, yielded himself faithfully into the Mercy; when he who was the Mercy dissolved into the Mercy, *in that exact moment the Mercy became one with the body of Christ.* From then on and ever hereafter the Mercy wears a human face—and that is the face of Christ.

If you can feel the explosion, the nuclear fusion that must have happened in this moment still reverberating in your own innermost ground, then you will be able to share in the intuition of the great mystics: that the Mercy, which we experience here as power, intelligence, purposive goodness, is really none other than the mystical body of Christ of which we are, inevitably and inalienably, living cells. The body of Christ, the body of hope, the Mercy: they are all one and the same thing. They are the unknown heart of God flung outward into accessible form so that nothing contained within that great outpouring can ever be lost or disappear—no idea, no possibility, no creature, no loved one. Nothing is ever lost. The root energy of love sustaining all, the light which drives creation and the light by which we know it, become one in Christ.

75

In that realization we reach the bedrock of mystical hope. And the third and greatest Mystery of the Mercy.

or depth of reverberating sound which surrounds like Tibetan pipes or monks voices

five

Hope and the Future

Hope is not something subjective due to an optimistic or sanguine temperament, or a desire for compensation in the sense of modern Freudian or Adlerian psychology. It is a light-force which radiates objectively and which directs creative evolution toward the world's future. It is the celestial and spiritual counterpart of terrestrial and natural instincts of biological reproduction.... In other words, hope is what moves and directs spiritual evolution in the world.

Valentin Tomberg

This powerful, challenging paragraph from Valentin Tomberg, the great French hermeticist[1], is really a meditation in itself and will essentially furnish the outline of my concluding chapter. For those not familiar with Valentin Tomberg, he was a Russian-born intellectual who became a great leader in European esoteric circles in the mid-twentieth century. Toward the end of his life (he died in 1973), Tomberg gravitated back to his Christian roots and wrote *Meditations on the Tarot,* a work that was originally published anonymously. The book represents a brilliant synthesis of esoteric and mystical wisdom. It was first introduced to me, incidentally, by Thomas Keating, who called it "the greatest contribution to date to the recovery of the Christian contemplative tradition."

In the above quotation, then, Tomberg calls attention to two aspects of mystical hope. The first is its orientation toward the future—toward evolution. In other words, he takes seriously that the world is going somewhere, and that hope is the means by which it gets there. Second, he claims that hope is objective—and thus, by inference, *public.* It does not have to do with our own private agendas, or even our subjective need for healing and empowerment. But it does have to do with moving us toward where *it* is going. Ultimately, hope is divine energy and intelligence moving toward the accomplishment of its purposes: it makes use of us rather than we of it.

79

The Future?

Perhaps you are confused at this point. At the beginning of the book I said that mystical hope is not about the future, but about the present. But now, along with Valentin Tomberg, I seem to be saying that it *is* about the future. How can both statements be true?

They can both be true when we shift our perspective from hope-as-object to hope-as-subject. In our usual way of thinking, as I said before, hope is tied to outcome; it is a feeling that arises when we experience ourselves moving toward the object of our desiring. (This is what I mean by hope-as-object.) And in this sense, as the Buddhists properly warn us, this kind of hope is illusory and disappointing because inevitably it takes us outside ourselves, when *inside ourselves* is where we need to be to discover the real wellsprings of hope.

But the nature of a wellspring is to spring forth. The nature of hope is to move, and to move forward. As subject—a force in its own right—it moves toward the future, carrying both itself and us toward deeper and more authentic manifestation.

Unlike the eastern religions, which tend to see reality as a return to the unitive source, the set of the western religions is toward the future, into new becoming. The body of Christ is not just a timeless, eternal reality, but moves through time in order to bring all things to their fulfillment in love.

In a simple, utterly practical way, that was the point my friend Jamien was trying to make in her deathbed instructions to her sons. When we are in a true way of being—that is, attuned to the homing beacon of our innermost ground, of the *point vierge*—hope is the current that flows through, carrying us toward the future. As we let ourselves yield and go with it, it will open us toward the authentic unfolding of our being. The opposite is also just as true: any form of resistance, be it nostalgia, clinging, bitterness, self-pity, or self-justification, will make it impossible to find that current of hope, impossible for hope to carry us to our true becoming. We become stones in the riverbed. But as far as we are able to yield, we yield objectively into hope.

Inner and Outer

I have spoken quite a lot in this book about the innermost ground; in fact, you could say that I have located the wellsprings of hope at the very center of our being, in that ground normally accessed through deep prayer and meditation. In this I realize there may be some conflict. Many Christians are suspicious of the whole interior landscape; they view contemplative prayer as private—even narcissistic—and feel that Christians who are truly concerned about the future should be spending less time meditating and more time saving the world.

A friend of mine in Colorado felt this way very strongly. A passionate social activist who would periodically seek sanctuary at the monastery in Snowmass between stints in jail for radical social action, he had nothing but contempt for the contemplative prayer movement. "Upper middle class navel-gazing," he called it.

It is true that contemplative prayer is often, even typically, presented in the language of personal healing and self-discovery: I enter stillness in order to purify my unconscious, heal the emotional wounds of a lifetime, find my true self, and so on. But there is a natural self-corrective mechanism built right into the prayer itself if we are willing to take it far enough: *my true self is found only in communion with others*. The personal can find its identity only in relation to the whole, which is the mercy of God.

We saw how Thomas Merton discovered this truth in his own blinding epiphany at the corner of 4th and Walnut in Louisville, when he suddenly found himself staring straight at the love that bound him and all these strangers together as fellow members of the human race. "It was like waking from a dream of separateness," he writes. His joy overflowing, he continues, "Thank God I *am* like other men!" And even his profound exposition of the *point vierge* that concludes this essay resonates with the same sense of awakening into Oneness. For Merton, the *point vierge* is not a private seat of individuality, a refuge from the darkness and cruelty of the world. In his words:

It is in everybody, and if we could see it we
would see these billions of points of light
coming together in the face and blaze of a
sun that would make all the darkness and
cruelty of life vanish altogether.[2]

Merton had experienced for himself that core
wisdom of the Trinity: in the innermost ground,
divine being is communal, self-communicating.
And because our true self is rooted in that divine
ground, it can never be found in pure emptiness,
as so often depicted in contemplative literature,
but only through pure *self-emptying* in love. As
we converge toward the *point vierge*, our illusion
of separate selfhood dissolves in something
greater and shared. The higher up the ladder of
spiritual progress we go, the more we know indis-
putably that we are a cell in the lifeblood of something infinitely greater.

"When you're a true hermit, you're never
alone," Rafe used to teach me. He lived out his
hermit's vocation in a small cabin under the side
of a mountain in what many would see as a life of
ultimate uninvolvement with the world. And yet
Rafe knew and lived the truth that hermits from
all ages have known and lived: that the solitary

work of prayer is ultimately communal, and in a powerful though mysterious way it upholds and maintains the life of this planet at an energetic level. Prayer, "piercing prayer"—as Julian of Norwich, another legendary hermit called it— affects something mightily. It pierces to the heart of God, like a strong electric current coursing through the Mercy, subtly rearranging and revivifying everything. Rafe was so convinced that the real work of prayer was done at this level that he used to say, only half-jokingly, that the principal job of a hermit was to "help maintain the spiritual ozone level of the planet."

Rafe taught me one other thing, which I will come back to later in this chapter. He used to say, "No conscious act is ever wasted." He believed that the quality of his attention in the way he changed a tire on his old Scout or recovered from a burst of anger could palpably change the quality of life on the planet. Pure acts of compassion or attention always affect something at the planetary level, he felt; they always change the course of events subtly but unmistakably.

A Metaphysics of Hope

Only recently have we Christians begun to feel even vaguely comfortable talking about things in this way, at the level of spiritual energy. The problem, essentially, as we approach this important issue of contemplative prayer and compassionate action is that we are working with an outgrown metaphysics. You could say we are still using a Newtonian theology in a quantum universe. While science has long since acclimated to thinking of matter and energy as one continuous field, in our older theological categories we still keep matter and energy rigidly separate—and God the most separate of all. Body and spirit are different. Creator and creature are different. We still do not know, apart from calling it pantheism, how to talk about God being in all things; how to speak of the substance (not merely the image) of divine life coursing through both the visible and the invisible in one continuous revelation of divine love. We keep trying to express a vision of unity within a metaphysics of separateness. What is needed is a "quantum" leap forward into a new way of seeing, just as happened to Thomas Merton on the corner of 4th and Walnut, so that we no longer focus on the separate things, but stare directly into the energy field that contains them all—that great "electromagnetic field of love," as Kabir Helminski called it.

It is something of this notion that I have been trying to develop throughout this book, not by delving into modern physics (although one finds plenty of confirmation there), but by exploring the visionary insights at the heart of Christian mysticism. And from the composite picture emerging from the Greek patristic fathers, from Jacob Boehme and Thomas Merton, from Julian of Norwich, Hildegard von Bingen, and Barbara Brown Taylor, and from so many Christian novelists and poets, I have tried to suggest a new way of picturing hope. In this new positioning, the underlying sense of corporateness is physically real, for that "electromagnetic field of love" is the Mercy—and the Mercy is the body of Christ. Through this body hope circulates as a lifeblood. It warms, it fills, it connects, it directs. It is the heart of our own life and the heart of all that lives.

Hope's home is at the innermost point in us, and in all things. It is a quality of aliveness. It does not come at the end, as the feeling that results from a happy outcome. Rather, it lies at the beginning, as a pulse of truth that sends us forth. When our innermost being is attuned to this pulse it will send us forth in hope, regardless of the physical circumstances of our lives. Hope fills us with the strength to stay present, to abide in the flow of the Mercy no matter what outer storms assail us. It is entered always and only through surrender; that is, through the willingness to let go of everything we are presently clinging to. And yet when we enter it, it enters *us* and fills us with its own life—a quiet strength beyond anything we have ever known.

And since that strength is, in fact, a piece of God's purposiveness coursing like sap through our own being, it will lead us in the right way. It sweeps us along in the greater flow of divine life as God moves—and in the western religions, God *does* move—toward the fulfillment of divine purpose which is the deeper, more intense, more subtle, more intimate revelation of the heart of God.

The Quality of Aliveness

In a remarkable account from her years spent in Africa, Isak Dinesen tells the story of how one day out in the bush she was fascinated by a beautiful snake, its skin glistening with subtle, variegated colors. She raved so much about that snakeskin that one of her house servants killed the snake, skinned it, and made it up into a belt for her. To her great dismay that once glistening skin was now just dull and gray. For all along the beauty had lain not in the physical skin but in the quality of its aliveness.

I use this story to return very practically to the question of hope and right action in the world. Christians almost from the start have been intent upon the mission of "building a new heaven and a new earth." And yet we have to admit that these new heavens and new earths, in layer upon layer of wreckage, never seem to stay put very long. So often our best efforts to further the reign of peace and justice on earth only wind up in burnout and disillusionment—and sometimes in far more serious backlashes. The kingdom of heaven, it seems, is never quite the same thing as an earthly utopia.

St. Brendan had to learn this lesson, too—that Irish navigator monk I mentioned in the first chapter. For seven years he circled in vain searching for an earthly paradise, the Land Promised to the Saints. Only when his eyes were finally opened did he see that the paradise he was seeking was literally "right beneath his nose." But it was a world within a world—not the physical place itself, but a quality of aliveness within it. Like Isak Dinesen's snakeskin, the land itself was merely the outer shell; it was the live holiness dancing within it that created the beauty.

The ancient Hebrews had a very strong way of picturing this live holiness. They called it "righteousness," as, for example, in Isaiah: "See, a king will reign in righteousness" (32:1); and in the Psalms: "He restores my soul; he guides me in paths of righteousness" (23:3). By "righteousness" they did not mean a moral template they could use to build an ideal replica of God's kingdom. They meant an energy-charged sphere—a forcefield, as we would express it in modern terms—in which all their plans, efforts, and schemes had to move in order to come to fruition. The innermost and the outermost had to be total-

ly "in sync." If so, a person had "purity of heart";
he or she was righteous—or as the term is more
accurately translated, "in the righteousness of
God." Otherwise, no efforts undertaken out of
one's own righteousness (one's own personal
forcefield), no matter how cleverly they simulated
the outward action, could possibly be worthy
because the crucial element was missing: the aliveness of God moving in it.

This ancient spiritual wisdom is still just as
timely today. Insofar as we are able to remain
simply and warmly within "the righteousness of
God," we are able to move out into the world as
agents of transformation, as creative channels of
God's own existential set toward the future. And
hope flows through us in precisely the way that
Valentin Tomberg describes: it "moves and directs
spiritual evolution in the world."

When there is a discrepancy, however—when
means do not match ends—the flow is interrupt-
ed, and the energy becomes confused. In an older
style of Christian social activism focused exclu-
sively on outer results it might be possible to over-
look this clash, but in a metaphysic geared to
quality of aliveness as the place where the work is

really being done, the dissonance becomes immediate and unbearable. If I say I am working for peace but am myself angry and self-righteous, then the energy I am putting into the atmosphere is anger and self-righteousness. If I come preaching the gospel of Christian love but am myself rigid and judgmental, I am putting into the atmosphere rigidity and judgment.

91

From the first century onward there has been a subterranean but distinct vein of Christianity known as the "inner tradition." In contrast to the mainstream, which came to emphasize doctrinal correctness and institutional loyalty, the inner tradition kept its focus squarely on the path of inner awakening taught and modeled by Christ. This vein of understanding flows from the *Gospel of Thomas* through the desert fathers and mothers and the spirituality of the Orthodox monks of Mount Athos, reemerges in the Protestant west in the teachings of Jacob Boehme and his followers, and continues to be represented in our own times in such voices as Valentin Tomberg and Helen Luke. Spiritual teachings in the inner tradition are adamant on the point I have just made. The energy accompanying an action is objectively real; it powerfully affects the field in which the action plays out (even if we are completely unaware of what we are "putting out"), and it will ultimately carry the day. A right action done with a wrong energy will ultimately become a wrong action. And because of the discrepancy between means and ends, the action will ultimately self-cancel, following the precept Jesus laid down in the gospel: "A house divided against itself will fall" (Luke 11:17).

92

Jacob Boehme, for one, was particularly insistent upon this point. What I have called "the righteousness of God" he calls "the will of God," but the underlying message is the same: the need for a strict congruency between means and ends. In *The Way to Christ* he teaches emphatically:

> No work outside of God's will can reach God's kingdom. It is all only a useless carving in the great laboriousness of man. Whatever occurs through the conclusions of the human self...is only a mirror of the contending wheel of nature where good and evil contend with one another. What good builds up, evil breaks down; and what evil builds up, good breaks down.

This is the great sorrow of useless labori-
ousness.[3]

Boehme was writing in religious times not
unlike our own, at the end of the first century of
the Protestant Reformation when the once-mono-
lithic Catholic Church was splintering into rival
denominations, and his words throw down a real
gauntlet to the church today. If mainstream
Christianity has steadily lost force and credibility
in the contemporary world—a fact that now
seems beyond denying—I wonder how much of
this decline might be attributed to the fact that for
so long now the means have not matched the
ends. We preach one gospel and live another. And
while in a way this has always been true, the clash
is accentuated in the security-obsessed consciousness of our own times. We preach the Good
Samaritan and lock our church doors. We preach
the lilies of the field and allocate large amounts of
our monthly paychecks to pension and insurance
plans. We preach forgiveness and trust and do
routine background checks on prospective priests
and church workers. Whatever we may think we
are up to in terms of furthering the reign of
Christ, what we are *actually* putting into the

atmosphere are fear, greed, stress, power and control issues—same as any other organization. Is it any wonder that hope fails us and the church is not taken seriously?

The Power of Integrity

94

Like Dorothy in *The Wizard of Oz,* the power is there all along, unsuspected but right on our own two feet. It is the power of integrity. If we really wish to change the planet, to become a sign of hope in a broken world, all we really need to do (and it is one simple thing, but it is everything) is to narrow the gap between means and ends: between the gospel we profess and the gospel we live out, moment to moment, in the quality of our aliveness. St. Francis, St. Anthony, Julian of Norwich, Dorothy Day, Mahatma Gandhi, Oscar Romero, Henri Nouwen: have not all these saints and "ones who got there" pointed us in exactly the same direction, toward the power of simple integrity? As Rafe said, "No conscious act is ever wasted." No unified, consistent energy generated by closing the gap between means and ends ever fails to change the world.

One who has lived this truth outstandingly in our own times is Frère Roger Schutz, founder of the Taizé Community in southeastern France, a place that has been called "a little miracle." Every year tens of thousands of people, particularly young people, come there from all over the world to pray and study scripture together. They live in barrack-like accommodations or camp out in tents, eat plain food served up mess hall style, and take their turns with the enormous workload of cooking, cleaning, and maintenance needed to keep this army of pilgrims marching forward. There are no frills and no corners cut; it is pure gospel Christianity. And in this atmosphere of simplicity, service, and deep prayer, the Christ light shines very brightly.

Each year the brothers of the community, who now number more than ninety, spend some time away from the monastery living among the world's radically poor. They do not go to engage in work projects or even to teach, but simply to be among the poor "as a sign of hope." The gift they bring is merely the gift of presence. But since that presence has its roots in the deepest ground of integrity and love, it cannot help but flow forth as hope.

I know something about the power of this presence, for it was a brief encounter with Frère Roger nearly thirty years ago that set me on the Christian path. In 1973, then a young graduate student, I traveled to Riverside Church in New York City to hear Frère Roger address the Trinity Institute. So moved was I by his beautiful, simple words of prayer that at the end of his talk, in spite of myself, I found myself joining the throng swelling forward.to meet him.

As the wave of people carried me steadily toward him, my panic increased. What would I say when I actually got there? Would I try to tell him all about myself in thirty seconds? Or the opposite—would I just stand there flustered and tongue-tied, wasting his time?

The line lurched forward and I was suddenly dumped into his presence. And there something happened that I would never have expected, and that changed my life forever. He simply looked at me, his beautifully gentle blue eyes right on me, and asked with tenderness, "What is your name?"

"Cynthia," I said.

"Oh, it is a lovely name," he said, and he looked deeply into me and through me, into depths I never even knew were there. For the next thirty seconds, I had his full attention—perhaps the first time this had ever happened to me in my life, the first time I had ever experienced what it means to be unconditionally loved. I left that encounter with my heart overflowing with hope; by the following year I was baptized. And it was nothing he said—just the power of the way he was present, his complete transparency to love. The Community of Taizé may be a miracle, but there is no secret behind this miracle: in the heart of its founder, deep prayer and compassionate action have become fused as one.

And this brings me back to the point where this chapter begins: that false and damaging dichotomy between inner and outer, between contemplation and action. For what holds us back from unified action is fear, and fear, as we saw in chapter three, is the inevitable product of being trapped in that smaller, isolated self; of being in "egoic consciousness." It takes enormous courage to live the Christian gospel, which is so quintessentially a path of "dying before you die." It takes tremendous courage to move forward in hope, knowing "Whether I live or die, I am the Lord's."

This courage is beyond the capacity of the ego, and a Christianity lived only ego-deep will ultimately betray itself.

But in the contemplative journey, as we swim down into those deeper waters toward the wellsprings of hope, we begin to experience and trust what it means to lay down self, to let go of ordinary awareness and surrender ourselves to the mercy of God. And as hope, the hidden spring of mercy deep within us, is released in that touch and flows out from the center, filling us with the fullness of God's own purpose living itself into action, then we discover within ourselves the mysterious plenitude to live into action what our ordinary hearts and minds could not possibly sustain. In plumbing deeply the hidden rootedness of the whole, where all things are held together in the Mercy, we are released from the grip of personal fear and set free to minister with skillful means and true compassion to a world desperately in need of reconnection.

Hope is not imaginary or illusory. It is that sonar by which the body of Christ holds together and finds its way. If we, as living members of the body of Christ, can surrender our hearts, reenter the righteousness, and listen for that sonar with all we are worth, it will again guide us, both individually and corporately, to the future for which we are intended. And the body of Christ will live, and thrive, and hold us tenderly in belonging.

Endnotes

Chapter 1: Journey to the Wellsprings
1. Kabir Helminski, *Living Presence: A Sufi Way to Mindfulness and the Essential Self* (New York: Jeremy Tarcher, 1992), 26.
2. Cynthia Bourgeault, *Love Is Stronger Than Death* (New York: Bell Tower, 1999).

Chapter 2: Living in the Mercy
1. Lynn C. Bauman, ed., *Ancient Songs Sung Anew* (Telephone, Tex.: Praxis, 2000), 258.

2. Helen M. Luke, *Old Age* (New York: Parabola Books, 1987), 84.

3. Ibid., 8.

4. Thomas Merton, *A Merton Reader,* ed. Thomas P. McDonnell (New York: Image Books, 1989), 351.

5. Ibid., 353

6. Barbara Brown Taylor, *The Luminous Web: Essays on Science and Religion* (Cambridge, Mass.: Cowley Publications, 2000), 74.

7. Ibid.

8. Jacob Boehme, *The Way to Christ* (Mahwah, N.J.: Paulist Press, 1978).

9. Gerald May, *Will and Spirit* (San Francisco: Harper and Row, 1982), 172.

10. Helminski, *Living Presence*, 118.

11. Matthew Fox, ed., *Breakthrough: Meister Eckhart's Creation Spirituality in New Translation* (New York: Image Books, 1980), 126.

12. From *Conjectures of a Guilty Bystander,* quoted in Merton, *A Merton Reader,* 345.

13. Ibid., 347.

102

14. Quoted in Rob Baker and Gray Henry, eds., *Merton and Sufism: The Untold Story* (Louisville: Fons Vitae, 1999), 64.

Chapter 3: Meditation and Hope
1. Thomas Keating, *Open Mind, Open Heart* (Rockport, Mass.: Element, 1996).

Chapter 4: Dying Before You Die
1. You may find this practice thoroughly described in the writings of Thomas Keating and in Bruno Barnhart's remarkable book *Second Simplicity* (Mahwah, N.J.: Paulist Press, 1999); it is a mainstay of Benedictine spirituality.

2. *Babette's Feast,* prod. Just Betzer and Bo Christensen, dir. Gabriel Axel, 103 min., Panorama Film International, 1987, videocassette.

3. Dylan Thomas, *Collected Poems* (New York: New Directions, 1957), 117.

4. Leo Tolstoy, *The Death of Ivan Ilych, and Other Stories,* A Signet Classic (New York: The New American Library, 1960), 154, 156.

5. Helminski, *Living Presence,* 128.

6. Thomas Merton, "True Freedom," transcribed from the cassette series *Sufism: Longing for God* (Kansas City: Credence Cassettes, 1995).

Chapter 5: Hope and the Future

1. Valentin Tomberg, *Meditations on the Tarot* (Rockport, Mass.: Element, 1993), 471-72. A hermeticist is one who pursues the ancient art of alchemy, not in order to turn lead into gold, but as a precise though veiled science of inner spiritual transformation.

2. Merton, *A Merton Reader*, 347.

3. Boehme, *The Way to Christ*, 123-24.

Water images - p 39 / well, river, ocean   25 - Swimming , 29·30

Immortal Love - Forever Full 64·66 - The fullness of